2. Barrier Reef

3. Cap'n Jack's Hornpipe

Double Bass

String Time Joggers

14 pieces for flexible ensemble

Kathy and David Blackwell

Contents

OXFORD

Sea Suite

1. Shark attack!

Printed in Great Britain

OXFORD UNIVERSITY PRESS, MUSIC DEPARTMENT, GREAT CLARENDON STREET, OXFORD OX2 6DP

Jazz Suite

4. Simple syncopation

Happy ♩ = 112

5. Feelin' blue

Slow and moody ♩ = 68

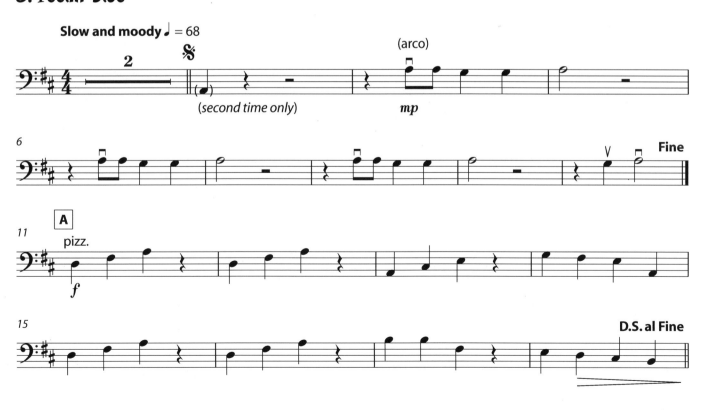

6. Broadway or bust

Jamaican Suite

7. Tinga Layo

West Indian Trad.

8. Jamaican lullaby

Jamaican Trad.

9. Kingston Calypso

Hollywood Suite

10. Spy movie 2

11. Sad movie

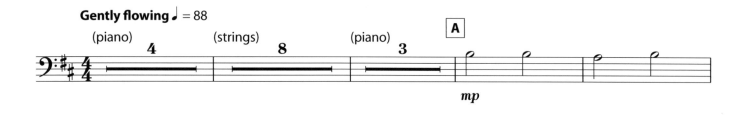

12. Action movie

Extras

13. Cowboy song

14. Banuwa

String Time Joggers

Kathy and David Blackwell

This exciting new series by the authors of *Fiddle Time*, *Viola Time*, and *Cello Time* provides great new ensemble material for all string groups, whatever their size. *String Time Joggers* is a must-have for all those looking for imaginative and enjoyable ensemble repertoire.

- 14 fun and characterful ensemble pieces—arranged in suites for concert performance
- CD with performances and backings for all pieces
- Flexible scoring for violin, viola, cello, and double bass with piano or CD accompaniment— from two parts to massed string ensemble!
- Pieces may also be played as solos for violin, viola, or cello, with piano or CD backing
- Lively illustrations in the pupils' books
- Corresponds to the level of *Fiddle Time Joggers*, *Viola Time Joggers*, and *Cello Time Joggers*— part 1 uses all fingers, part 2 uses 0–1 only

Teacher's pack
Includes full score, piano score,
notes on the pieces, and CD
(ISBN 978-0-19-335916-1)

Violin book with CD
(ISBN 978-0-19-335913-0)

Viola book with CD
(ISBN 978-0-19-335914-7)

Cello book with CD
(ISBN 978-0-19-335915-4)

Double Bass part (excl. CD)
(ISBN 978-0-19-335970-3)

You can look at and listen to pieces from the *String Time Joggers* books at
www.oup.com/uk/music/stringtime

OXFORD

UNIVERSITY PRESS

www.oup.com

Illustrated by Andy Hammond

ISBN 978-0-19-335970-3

9 780193 359703